D1482962

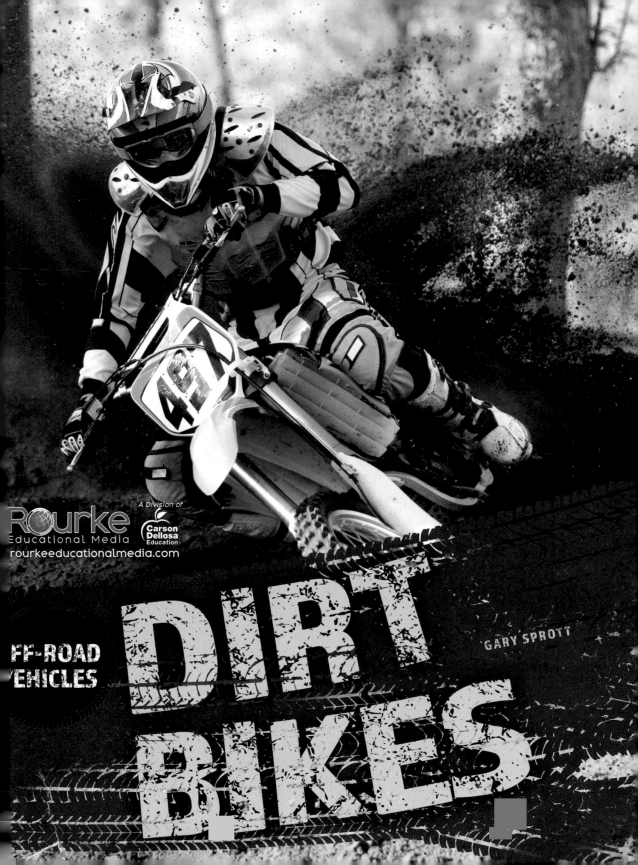

Rourke
Educational Media

rourkeeducationalmedia.com

A Division of
Carson Dellosa
Education

FF-ROAD
'EHICLES

DIRT
BIKES

GARY SPROTT

Before Reading: *Building Background Knowledge and Vocabulary*

Building background knowledge can help children process new information and build upon what they already know. Before reading a book, it is important to tap into what children already know about the topic. This will help them develop their vocabulary and increase their reading comprehension.

Questions and Activities to Build Background Knowledge:

1. Look at the front cover of the book and read the title. What do you think this book will be about?
2. What do you already know about this topic?
3. Take a book walk and skim the pages. Look at the table of contents, photographs, captions, and bold words. Did these text features give you any information or predictions about what you will read in this book?

Vocabulary: *Vocabulary Is Key to Reading Comprehension*

Use the following directions to prompt a conversation about each word.

- Read the vocabulary words.
- What comes to mind when you see each word?
- What do you think each word means?

Vocabulary Words:
- acrobatics
- agile
- maintain
- priority
- recreation
- suspension

During Reading: *Reading for Meaning and Understanding*

To achieve deep comprehension of a book, children are encouraged to use close reading strategies. During reading, it is important to have children stop and make connections. These connections result in deeper analysis and understanding of a book.

 ### Close Reading a Text

During reading, have children stop and talk about the following:

- Any confusing parts
- Any unknown words
- Text to text, text to self, text to world connections
- The main idea in each chapter or heading

Encourage children to use context clues to determine the meaning of any unknown words. These strategies will help children learn to analyze the text more thoroughly as they read.

When you are finished reading this book, turn to the next-to-last page for **After Reading Questions** and an **Activity**.

TABLE OF CONTENTS

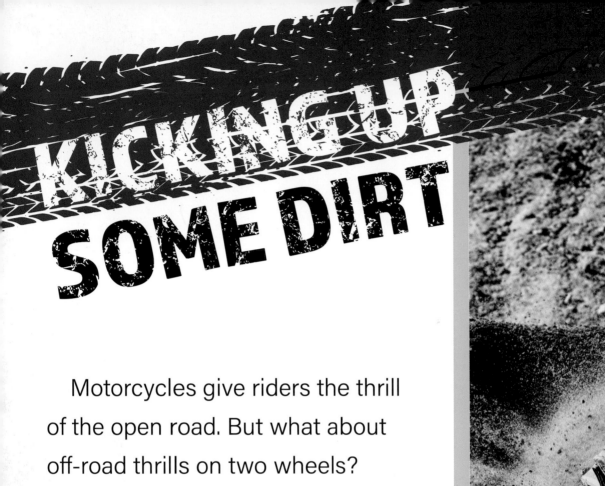

KICKING UP SOME DIRT

Motorcycles give riders the thrill of the open road. But what about off-road thrills on two wheels? Welcome to the rip-roaring, trailblazing world of dirt bikes!

Tykes on Bikes!

Children as young as four years old compete in dirt bike motocross races! These mini-racers ride mini-motors on tracks and cross-country trails.

Dirt bikes are lighter than regular motorcycles. That makes them more **agile** for handling off-road conditions. It also means they are less likely to get stuck in the mud!

agile (AJ-il): able to move quickly and easily

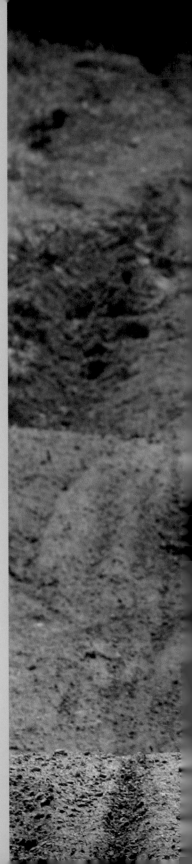

They may be light, but they're no lightweights! Dirt bikes have to be tough to survive punishing trails. A sturdy frame and a strong **suspension** are must-haves for bone-shaking jumps and landings.

suspension (suh-SPEN-shuhn): the mechanical system in a vehicle that has springs to keep the vehicle stable, to protect it from the road, and to help the driver maintain control

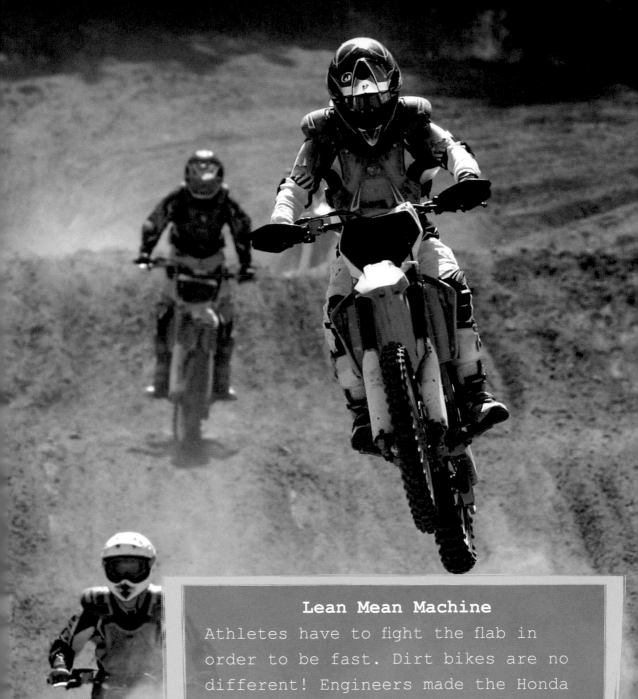

Lean Mean Machine

Athletes have to fight the flab in order to be fast. Dirt bikes are no different! Engineers made the Honda CRF450R lighter by getting rid of the kickstarter. Now this speedster is raring to go at the push of a button!

Dirt bike tires grip the ground like a python grips its prey! This super-strength traction allows riders to make tight turns on slippery mud or shifting sand.

Tread Carefully
Different tire treads can be used for different track or trail surfaces. Many dirt bike tires have big square knobs with deep ridges in between. These are nicknamed "knobbies."

There are two types of dirt bike engines: two-stroke and four-stroke. A *stroke* describes the movement of the pistons inside the engine as air and fuel are sucked in. A two-stroke engine is often lighter and can get the bike to higher speeds more quickly. A four-stroke engine gives a smoother ride.

There's an App for That!

The Yamaha YZ250F is a dirt bike techie! Riders can download Yamaha's Power Tuner app on their smartphone and program when they want to give their bikes more gas! This real-time fine-tuning is then uploaded through the bike's Wi-Fi system!

The KTM 250 has a two-stroke engine.

The KTM 450 has a four-stroke engine.

GEARING UP FOR FUN

Just because you're off-road doesn't mean there are no rules of the road to follow. Safety is the top **priority** for dirt bike riders. There's no fun in getting hurt.

priority (prye-OR-i-tee): something that is more important or more urgent than other things

On a Path to Success

Do you play a sport such as soccer, lacrosse, or basketball? You need coaching and practice to be successful, right? Well, learning to ride a dirt bike is no different.

Dirt bikes are powerful machines with many moving parts. Riders must **maintain** their bikes regularly and make necessary repairs. That keeps things running smoothly and safely.

maintain (mayn-TAYN): to keep something in good condition

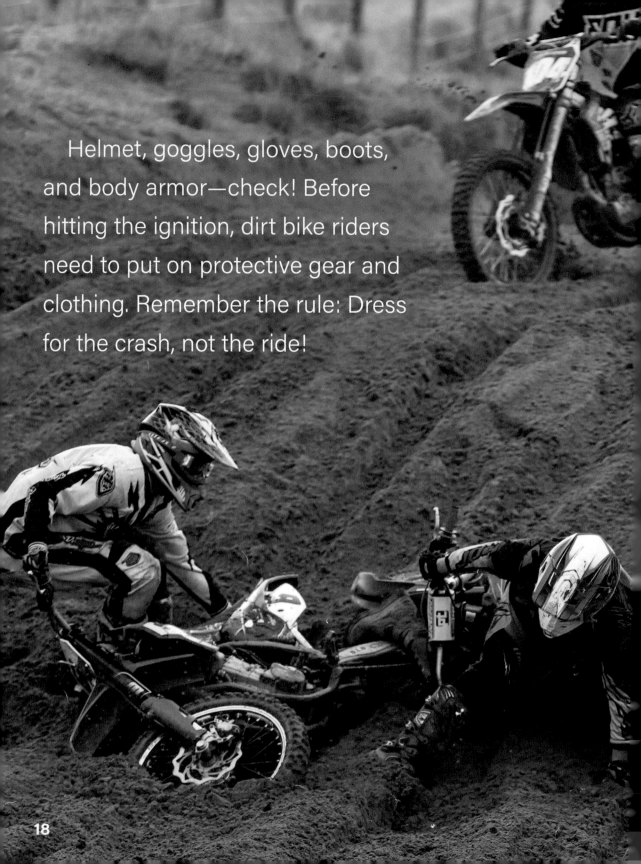

Helmet, goggles, gloves, boots, and body armor—check! Before hitting the ignition, dirt bike riders need to put on protective gear and clothing. Remember the rule: Dress for the crash, not the ride!

A Good Starting Point

Organizations such as the American Motorcyclist Association provide many resources about dirt bikes. Beginners and experienced riders can get tips on safety, racing, and maintenance.

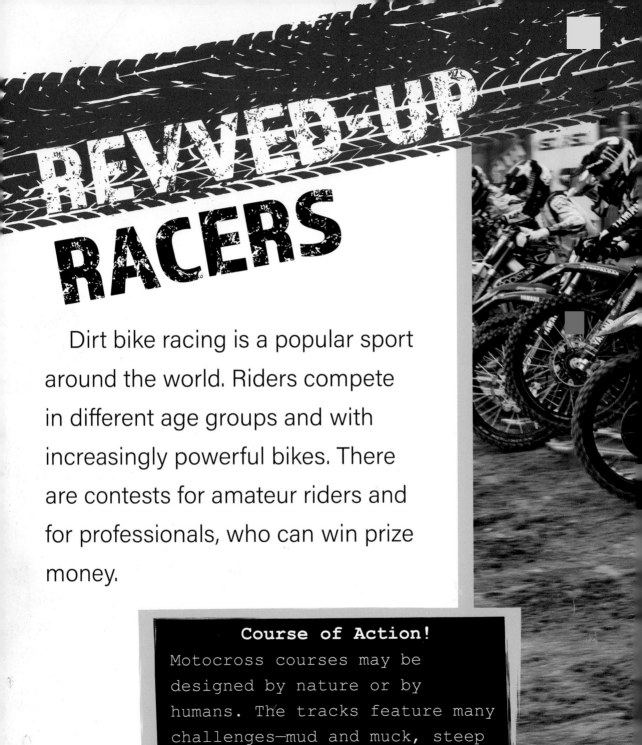

REVVED-UP RACERS

Dirt bike racing is a popular sport around the world. Riders compete in different age groups and with increasingly powerful bikes. There are contests for amateur riders and for professionals, who can win prize money.

Course of Action!

Motocross courses may be designed by nature or by humans. The tracks feature many challenges—mud and muck, steep hills, jumps and bumps, and sharp turns.

Motocross racing began in Europe just after World War II ended in 1945. In the 1970s, the sport grew in popularity in the United States. Japanese motorcycle manufacturers such as Honda, Suzuki, Yamaha, and Kawasaki began building dirt bikes in big numbers.

A French Connection

The name *motocross* comes from *motocyclette*—the French word for motorcycle—and *cross country*. Races are known as *motos*. Très bon!

Top riders perform gravity-defying **acrobatics** with their bikes. In midair, they whip their bike sideways so it seems to be flying like a Frisbee! Or they might flip their bikes head-over-heels like a stunt rider.

acrobatics (ak-ruh-BAT-iks): difficult gymnastic acts, often performed in the air or on a high wire

Motocross is just one type of dirt bike racing. Hare scrambles are cross-country races that take riders through forests, deserts, and other tough terrain. In extreme off-road racing, bike and rider must conquer a course covered in rocks, logs, and other obstacles.

You've Been Roosted!

Dirt bike racing has its own language. *Whoops* are bumps or mounds in a row. *Holeshot* is being the first rider to get to the first corner in a race. But don't get *roosted*—that means the bike in front is kicking dirt in your face!

Dirt bikes aren't just for racers. Weekend riders rev up their engines for off-road **recreation** and the thrill of the trail.

---

recreation (rek-ree-AY-shuhn): the games, sports, and hobbies that people enjoy in their spare time

Memory Game

Look at the pictures. What do you remember

reading on the pages where each image appeared?

Index

After Reading Questions

1. What is the top priority for dirt bike riders?

2. What are *whoops*?

3. Where did motocross racing begin?

4. Why is it important for dirt bikes to be light?

5. What is traction?

Activity

Design a dirt bike racing board game that works like Chutes and Ladders. Add different challenges to different squares and roll dice to move your playing piece. Did you land on the *roosted* square? Yikes! You have to move your piece backward.

About the Author

Gary Sprott is a writer in Tampa, Florida. He has written books about ancient cultures, animals, plants, and automobiles. Gary loves exploring new topics for his books. He's never been on a dirt bike, but now he knows how cool they are!

www.rourkeeducationalmedia.com

PHOTO CREDITS: Cover, page 1 : ©HStarr; pages 4-5, 30: ©PeopleImages; pages 5, 30: ©davidf; pages 6-7, 30: ©sportpoint; pages 8-9: ©jpbcpa; pages 10-11: ©Pavel1964; page 12: ©Phothoughts; page 13: ©RSchedl; page 15: ©Parilov / Shutterstock; pages 16-17, 30: ©Fertnig; pages 18-19, 30: ©Jasperimagescotland; pages 20-21: ©sippakorn, pages 22-23: ©Krusanit; pages 24-25: ©Sundownoel; pages 26-27: ©Robert Hoetink; pages 28-29, 30: ©Simonkr

Edited by: Kim Thompson
Cover and interior design by: Rhea Magaro-Wallace

Library of Congress PCN Data

Dirt Bikes / Gary Sprott
(Off-Road Vehicles)
ISBN 978-1-73161-456-8 (hard cover)
ISBN 978-1-73161-257-1 (soft cover)
ISBN 978-1-73161-561-9 (e-Book)
ISBN 978-1-73161-666-1 (ePub)
Library of Congress Control Number: 2019932458

Rourke Educational Media
Printed in the United States of America,
North Mankato, Minnesota